C'est *La* Vie

~that's life~

Tanisha Kaushik

C'est la vie
Tanisha Kaushik

Published by White Falcon Publishing
Chandigarh, India

The contents of this book have been certified and timestamped
on the Gnosis blockchain as a permanent proof of existence.
Scan the QR code or visit the URL given on the back cover
to verify the blockchain certification for this book.

ISBN - 979-8-89222-332-4

Acknowledgement

And then on one of those Saturday nights, I remember sitting among class 10th girls, reciting my poetries to them in their dorm. The ones who made me realize that I was capable of something like this.

A dream then, a reality now. There are many hands that have helped me in making this dream come true. All the poetries and proses of this book are entitled to some people who will stay forever with me, encapsulated within the eternal echo of these pages.

Many aspects of my life revolves around the gates of SelaQui. From my best to my worst, I have seen it all. SelaQui has cherished me with joy and awe that I will always be grateful for.

My biggest debt is to my parents, thank you for always guiding me and sorry for disappointing you ever so often.

My friends, Thank you Adrija, Udayan and Deepika for always being with me, through thick and thin, and listening to my poetries at the oddest hour of the day.

And a very special thanks goes to a beautiful lady, who has always supported me, and been with me throughout, Ms. Gwendoline O'Brien. Thank you so much ma'am.

My mentor and my backbone, Mr. Ashford Lyonette. Thank you so much sir for bringing out that poet in me. None of this would have been possible without you. And to the people who have despised me; thank you for always giving me reasons to rise higher after every fall.

Content

Content

My Way

Meandering through Life's complexities,
For solitude I stopped a while.
As the subconscious unraveled the past,
I oscillated between sigh and smile.

There I was in innocent bliss,
Too naive for the world to read.
A simple soul that couldn't discern,
Between thought and talk and deed.

Molded young, I realized,
The manipulative ways of man.
The cynical me can clearly see,
Foes amidst my clan.

This trade was certainly not by choice,
It was more by circumstance.
Perhaps another would have cried,
But I decided to dance.

The Sun, The Moon, The Glory

The moon is drunk and the night is high,
Stars all intoxicated, narrates the sky.
"What makes you drink so furious ?"
Asks the sea to the moon all curious.
Smiles the moon for the memories last,
As it had been a story of the past.

The moon replies, "For me to shine bright
The sun sets low; asking no questions despite
being the only reason for my glow tonight.
And look at me how selfish I've become,
I yet dream of dancing to the sky's rhythm.
The Sun cares less for her desires, but more for me,
Hoping in the dark, her sacrifice I'll see."

Role Reversal

Like driftwood in the lyrical sea,
I submerged in verse and creativity.
No Fairy Tale could I call to mind,
Where Spartan lasses saved princes kind.
Forbidden all challenges, denied all sin,
Virgin swords can't battles win.
The knight in armor is always male,
With brain and brawn and eye for detail.
Why can't a princess the dragon slay
rescue her prince and save the day?

The Poison of Your Wine

The poison of your wine,
An intoxicating brew.
The aroma fruity fine,
the flavor makes me new.

A portion each day I sip,
A measure, my pain to sooth.
And then my thankless lips,
Whisper words of gratitude.

No daunting day, me can break,
Irrespective of how the future's fated.
With each sip of your wine I take,
The living me seems invigorated.

Deep within there seems a doubt,
That causes much worry and pain.
If ever your wine does run out,
Would your poison ease my vein?

A Heart of Stone

Amidst the serenity of virtue,
Resides a heart of stone.
A quiet yet dangerous rebel,
Composed, though trauma prone.

This heart wasn't always peeved,
In birth it was essentially gentle.
For all those times it was grieved,
It's switched to sentimental.

Often too cold to desire,
As if a sedated heart.
Sometimes like raging forest fire,
Destroying all in its path.

These lethal flames to contain,
I'm mindful of my tone.
For it is the voices of disdain,
That turns a heart to stone.

If I Told You

If I told you about the darkness deep within,
Of the burden of guilt, despite not committing sin.
Would you still admire me, like the summer sun?

If I told you about the hidden scars,
The outcome of some sinister flaws in my stars.
Would you still fall for me like autumn leaves?

If I told you about my past, so cursed,
The parts I've played, unprepared, unrehearsed.
Would you still find me as pure as the winter snow?

If I told you of my thoughts that are at constant unrest,
Of my conviction that I do not deserve the best.
Would you still let me blossom in your spring?

Only if I told you...
Would you still?

In Her Eyes

She is there, just look into her eyes,
You'll know if you could read grief,
Her smiling facade of make-belief.

She has been bruised throughout,
Ask her about her happy memories
And watch her visage palely freeze.

If you should ask her where she goes,
She'd point to dark cozy haunts,
Where there are no murmur and no one taunts.

Her cheerful chirpiness camouflages,
The rainy nights that leave her drenched,
With a dizzy head and fists clenched.

She is not that learned; you could tell,
Thought her eyes are an angelic charm,
They've absorb over time and now are calm.

I Won't let you Go

'I wont let you go,' I say,
But life's complexities silently scream,
"It's a dream, only a dream."

'I wont let you go,' I say,
Then wear a persuasive pretense,
To cast aside consequence.

'I wont let you go,' I say,
For I'm certainly not yet prepared,
for the precariousness that lies ahead.

I wont let you go,' I say,
And tears deceive my eye,
Knowing someday will spell goodbye.

I wont let you go,' I say,
Then in reverence, I pray,
For the strength to walk away.

Demons

I've heard of demons, seen them too,
The most common walk midst me and you.
Disguised in dignity, virtuous of speech,
Ironically not practicing what they preach.

Demons were once angels divine and pure,
Cast out of heaven for misdemeanor.
They found themselves place among worldly ranks,
Using man's mind to implement their pranks.

Demons can praise, demons can woo,
Use much flattery to persuade you.
They are slowly crafted cause after cause.
I know my demons, do you know yours?

Strange! I like Pain

Strange enough, I like the pain,
Though it hurts, I resist complain.
Suffering seems to bring much delight,
Like bruises endured in a victorious fight.

Stranger still, the pain likes me,
It help me create through misery.
It's taught me to smile when I'm weak,
Put my neck on the line when fortune is bleak.

Crises situations sometimes I build,
That my desires are somehow fulfilled.
The more I'm quenched, the more I crave,
Like a surfer awaiting another wave.

Like toxic venom in my veins,
It comforts the heart and spurs the brains.
Many see this addiction as a curse,
For me its an inspiration to write verse.

I don't want Forever

I don't want forever,
For fantasy is quite bizarre.
What I do want however,
Is these moments just as they are.

I don't want forever,
Empty words spoken in vow.
Yet I earnestly endeavor,
To seize all that's for now.

I don't want forever,
For life itself is too short.
It's surely quite clever,
To make the most of what we've got.

I don't want forever,
Just some space in your time.
For no matter whatever,
I'll reminisce all that's sublime.

Eleven Eleven

A monochromatic soul entitled with the colors of heaven,
To them he was a man, but for me he was my 11:11.

A number of fortunes, believe is so and I wish to be true,
If it could bring him back even for little, throughout I'd choose.

This is a tale of a tryst of two, victim of misfortune;
one flew away,
But still protected her, within a tree of fringes
where his soul stayed.

In the midst of the forest as she sits down there,
Looking at that distant tree, merrily standing near the cut square.

The tree she'd sit under everyday after dusk all the way to set,
As it stretches its arm for her to rest.

She'd talk to him about her days and spend her night along,
Wishing for him, knowing this isn't where
he would anymore belong.

He would answer her with the swift rustle of the leaves,
Showering those little white flowers on her sleeves.

Love is in the company of his soul resonating to those fringes,
Who would still take care of her Under the roof of squinches.

But there is this ache in her heart, unable to heal,
As she, with an open heart prays to the almighty on her knees.

The little breeze touches her skin,
as she could recognize his breath,
For he committed himself to her entirely beyond
the gates of death.

She'd smile at ease, while inside longing to hug him once again,
Could picture clear the last moment of his,
the way his eyes reflected pain.

She was in love and so was he, more than
what could've held stitches seven,
For them she was a woman, but for him she was his 11:11.

The Aurora in You

Have you witnessed aurora?
The vivid amalgamation of colors
Abstract yet deep
Thronging with shades, yet empty
Light and dark
Dim and bright
Whirls turned cold white
Shades of purple and blue
Borders of gold coincide too

Just like your eyes
Not endless oceans but gracious skies
The elements of faded brown
Set in with dark hazel crown
Deeper than the depths of the core
Broader than the stretching shore
With passion that's blaring out
In totality, without doubt
Orbiting me like the moon
Causing an unremitting swoon
The hunger of your presence intense
Yearning to quench my suspense

Bygones

On the edge of a city, in an edifice grand,
Upon the roof top, in deep deliberation I stand.
Glancing at the glamorous town, vigorous at twilight,
My remedy, my escape, I put to lip, then light.

With each inhale and each exhale,
My thought fade from bright to pale.
Yesterday's mirage, isn't tomorrow's oasis,
Our past has vanished with faint traces.

Paths and priorities altered,
Not one, but both had faltered.
I wonder sometimes If it would be better,
If the both of us were in the same sweater.

A walk down memory lane is tough,
So I smudge bygones with another puff.

If ever Dreams come True

If it was a dream
I'd dream of you
My soul would be yours
And You'd love me too
I'd bathe in the delicacy of faith
For I'll know you are mine
At least I could dream,
For you're the dream I dream of
Marred with the jinx of reality.

In my wildest dreams,
Through the indistinct pathway of thrust
I charter to be your portal of ease.
From the shadowy glee of my soul
I adore the dimensions of your whorls.
I've taken a leap in the dark
Not I regret but I revere the now
For if it is a dream
I'd dream of you throughout.

Unconditional

Came to me in pleasure, in tears,
Bring with you your mirth, your fears.
Unravel each thought without restrain,
It's only me, you needn't feign.

At times stay coy at times be bold,
I'll be your comfort when the world appears cold.
I do not perceive, I will not judge,
I'll coax your wrath and bear no grudge.

Say 'sorry' if you think you must,
But above all give me your trust.
I'll neither critique nor idolize,
Till the time you realize,

Among the presence of provisional,
Somethings in life are 'unconditional'.

Dithered

I am messed up, a little too bad.
Maybe there's no love, but I still look for it.
Maybe there's love but I still can't find it.
I have lost my path, but I see you
Somewhere between the yellow of the yews.
Shall I wait?
Or shall I keep walking?
I am doubtful
Not of me,
But you.

I want you but you're presence
Feels heavy these days
I long for you but you're absence
No difference does it makes.
I want to sail through
But you make me drown
As I witnessed the fall out.
All I have are these barren words
And memories soon to be forgotten.
The drag to the low
And the darkness that cheers
Has left me weeping
With faded tears.

That June

Am I blurring out
Or are the miles feebly stretching?
The way years collapse
Like a dilapidated bridge into the river

Remember the fierce inference
'Our sun will shine too'.
Only to be betrayed by dawn in June.

The pain of that wreck
The vague figure of success
Departure of your love

The rebound of my heart
Breaking into halves
The condition of my soul?
Filled yet empty like a clock.

Cryptogenic Love of a Seraphic Lover

I'd invite you for a little walk,
On one of those nights with
Full moon hung low-high
And as we walk along
I'd talk to you, about
My ineffable love
In a tranquil crown,
I'd talk more about
All the swevens
Putting my hair down.

You're tall and beautiful
Flaming yet cute.
And those huge little eyes
As deep as the night sky.
I could see the verseluft
For your eyes are the
Window to the soul.
And those phosphenes
As the glare I behold.

Desiring of limerence
As the dulcet of your voice
Falls, in diligence.
Let us not deviate of purpose
For this is not a tryst,
Or it is?
As long as it stays with us.

This heart is pretty murk
For it had lost too much
Too conscious of being heard,
Yet, falling in, to voice each touch.
Of all the darkness
It dreams of the moon
Of all the voices
It dreams of your croons.

In the Guilt of Her Wreck

He is guilty of her wreck
Of a sin too humble to address
She was an independent dove
Caged in the name of love

Innocently far from worldly pleasures
For him she was inaccessible treasure
Every Time she walked down
Footsteps followed around

Naive was she to confide in him
He waited till the addiction did brim
And slowly, like opium's euphoric cure
His sadism made her feel more pure

He performed all shades of gray
Yet she couldn't walk away
Her soul and peace defenestrated
His exploitation unabated

Saturated with his craze
He left her in a daze
He still pays the bill in reality cheque
In the guilt of her wreck.

Roses and Thorns

The skin had gotten older,
Over the course of dawns.
I'd summarize her brief life,
Through roses and thorns.

Though a devotee of her swirls,
I often preach to her soul.
She taught me the art of living,
Making my vacuum whole.

The glamour, the beauty, the turmoil,
Gracefully met with advance and recoil.
A gradient of virtue, darkness to light,
Penitent when wrong, modest when right.

Despising and cherishing, a captive of thoughts,
Reminiscing the past, she unties their knots.
Surrendering to destiny and all the bygones,
Her life is a bouquet of roses and thorns.

By the River

My broken heart and me,
Sit by the river, melancholy.
I wonder, 'why we don't align?'
Me and this heart of mine.

My heart in love submerged,
And all those emotions surged.
But me, I knew the price,
Of not heeding to advice.

With affection came affliction,
Undesired contradiction.
Between my heart and me,
Induced by the baggage of misery.

The wreck was certainly fated,
Yet my heart's now disintegrated.
I curse my heart that aches,
For it makes the same mistakes.

My heart like the river flows,
For no boundaries it knows.
And me the cost must pay,
For allowing my heart to stray.

My trembling feet I tell,
'It was my heart, not me who fell'.
In the river I immerse to heal,
My broken heart to conceal

Story of the Wild

There are flowers that bloom at night.
She was one of them; beauty florescent
and vulnerable, too young to be called wise
Dreamt of dancing with the bees in the rain

To the little evil they turned her into
Might of a monster, body of a child
The damage ruined her right through
The fluorescence withered: sprouting a soul wild

And the beauty of her damages and the known
Taught her how to make hell feel like home.

Never Trust a Mirror

Never trust a mirror!
It makes you believe in things that don't exist.
It only shows you the outside making you feel worthy.

Never trust a mirror!
Can it see how your soul lights up
Caring not about the judgements and stares ?

Never trust a mirror!
It doesn't show you what the world sees
When you're only being you.

Never trust a mirror!
Can it see the paradox in you
How you can love everyone yet none?

Never trust a mirror!
And if you think it defines you
It's time to look within.

Two Sides

And just like the Moon he had a dark side,
To which even the Sun couldn't shine.
And from the shallow of his eyes,
I saw the craters, yielding sin,
Hiding slyly underneath his skin.

A sense of curiosity tickles,
For an arcane soul like him,
Had never crossed through.
Yet I could comprehend the brew.

I would take him to a quiet place,
Whistle down the chaos in wild blaze.
And suddenly he became my panacea,
A eutony of affection; curing me parts and bits.

A quixotic force I could sense very fierce,
Appealing to me, in ways so diverse.
Now me every moment high on his reverie,
For I could not stop gleaming at his divinity.

The Crescent

"What is love?" asked the moon
"It is the cause for my pale swoon?"
'Something that burns and brightens'.
Says the sun as it crosses the horizon.

"Don't listen to him." intervened the clouds'
"This ball of gas doesn't know what it's talking about",
rolling eyes at the sun as they furthered more.
The sun said 'Who but me makes the roses grow?'

"We do" argues the cloud; the rain in turn,
Makes the field green, and oceans run.
Nourishing with love and care,
"It's not just you but us in pair"

'Why'd you ask?' the sun inquires,
"I feel trapped between repulse and desires".
"I think I'm in love" the moon pondered
As the stars in the night sky twinkled and wandered.

"I love her ripples, I love her waves,
Placid to livid, the way she behaves.

Her blush when the sun goes down,
The way she drapes her azure gown."

'Bogus! The irate sun exclaimed,
I see her charm has you framed.
She blows my breath land to sea,
And that blush is her embracing me.'

Said the cloud, 'Its quite the flirt with me as well,
For it willingly absorbs my teary spell.
It conducts my wrath when I strike with light.
And turns my shade on a starless night.'

The blanched moon in silence sighed,
From full to crescent it shyly shied.

Remembering Aditya

And I'd sit in my veranda with a cup of tea,
Laying my eyes on the backyard, nostalgically.

Back to the days when three of us used to play around,
Catching those colored butterflies and beetles brown.

And you, the youngest, would say, "I'll protect you,
Don't be afraid, they are not that huge".

Back then when we were just kids. Four, twelve and fourteen,
Playing hide and seek, exploring all the corners unseen.

Time flew away, so did our childhood; leaving but memories,
And the night our lives changed, bashed up car upside
down on the field.

I'm Nineteen now, and your brother's eighteen.
All tall and grown.
About to graduate in a few weeks, and you happen to still be four.

Mom still looks for you around, around the house teary eyed.
And of all the places you chose those pictures to hide behind.

Sleeping over Confusion

In the quiet realm where dreams take flight,
A sanctuary found in the hush of night.
Beneath the crescent moon's soft diffusion,
I lay my head, seeking sleep's sweet illusion.

As the eyelids close, curtain descends,
Softly, uncertainty comprehends.
In the quietude of dreams, a refuge I find,
A shelter of peace for the restless mind.

Amidst the pillows my heart peeps,
The chaotic thoughts in my mind asleep.
Echoes of skepticism fill the air,
A symphony of chaos, a restless affair.

So, let me drift on the river of dreams,
Where clarity reigns in soothing streams.
Sleeping over confusion, a restful tide,
Guiding me gently to the morning's side.

Faces in the Crowd

A hundred faces or more, each day I see,
Anger, joy, sorrow, anxiety and misery.
There's a story each wants to convey,
If unheard now it will wither away.

The shades don't matter, the eyes do,
The emotions they transfer, not the hue.
Skin smooth and wrinkled of young and old,
From smiles contagious to brows that fold.

Who has the patience for thoughts of the head?
When the world is busy in earning their bread.
Yet in the crowd those faces I see,
For in them I find reflections of me.

Euthymia and Helios

Once upon an eternity in the vast expanse of the cosmos,
Bloomed a delicacy, nestled amidst the celestial meadows
Yearning for the warmth of connect, unfolding petals each
Euthymia, nor the universe serene could reach.

The other side of cosmos, resided the mighty Helios, the sun,
His golden beam traversed the cosmos, burning every turn.
Euthymia, captivated by the distant glow, yearning for love,
That transcended celestial boundaries, miles away miles above.

One day, in a cosmic waltz portrayed by fate,
Helios cast his radiant gaze upon the tempest soul weight.
His warmth caressed her petals, embroidering was the plan
And the dance of love between the flower and the sun began.

The sun marveled at the flower's resilience as she embraced
The rays of gentle calm, along restless storms she traced.
Transcended the boundaries of time and space,
Basked in the heat of the sun, stunned in a wild blaze.

Euthymia's petals mirrored the hues of the sunrise and sunset,
Helios painted the celestial canvas with thoughts so modest.
Yet, as with all tales in the cosmic tapestry, challenges emerged,
The flower, grounded in the celestial soil, deeply yearned.

Bound to illuminate the cosmos, couldn't alter the cosmic laws,
The sun, known to desires presented the gift of perpetual cause
The flower, now radiant with the sun's essence,
Continued to bloom, casting her light in sun's presence.

Their love story unfolded as a timeless parable,
The flower and the sun, kind of love, non malleable.
A testament to the profound philosophy
Even in the vast wild, love finds its own cosmic choreography.

Moonlit Eyes

Beneath a sky where twilight bleeds to night,
We stand, two souls stitched in irenic light.
Your hand in mine, two poetries held close,
Unfolding verses where darkness glows.

Whispered nothing, whispered all,
Just moonlit eyes, and the delight fall.
I trace your stars, constellations beyond,
Map my heart upon your skin, souls correspond.

No fear of dawn, no shadows cast ahead,
This stolen moment, a memory I wish never shed.
For love's a firefly, ephemeral flame,
That flickers bright, then fades, leaving no name.

Yet in its gentle, a fleeting truth is spun,
A whispered verse, sung beneath the sun.
And though this night may end, this love will be,
A phantom echo, echoing forever in me.

This rhyme, I envy and admire,
Born from moments, fueled by fire,
Shall sleep with shadows, may not be told,
A secret poem, your eyes behold.

If I Could

I wish I could but I'm afraid it's too late
If I could I would make him craft a new fate

Met me on the best days, met me on the worst
I want to hold, but this haze of love will soon burst
Broken would be two, a heart of yours, a heart of mine
Shattered would be two, a soul of yours, a soul of mine.

I wish I could take you back to the night we met
The night where promises were told to be kept.

The Threshold

The threshold is near, and I must cross,
Encouraging possibility taunts irrecoverable loss.
Hurtling through time in the greed of more,
Poetries and stories, known only to those walls four.

Two years too brief, two years too long,
With lingering memories like the words of a song.
Lives fated to converge, but not to stay,
Ballet orchestrated by love, harmony led the way.

Recognition and indifference I wittingly faced,
Some bonds fortified, some connections replaced.
In the quietest hour, hopes were whispered in the ear,
Amidst the blaze of chaos, the only voice I would hear.

Pages need to be turned, for the story must go on,
Teary hearts, afraid of the echoes of dawn.
Time is too principled to borrow or lend.
The threshold is near, this journey must end.

Quotes

If I were to be the earth
You would've been my big bang theory,
Unreal yet magical.

No matter how many words I put through the thread,
it will never be enough to bead my love for you.

In the quiet surrender of his last moment,
he found unexpected peace,
leaving behind a tale that echoes
in the heart of those who remember him.

*Had we known what tomorrow holds
would we be on tenterhooks tonight?*

I am homesick for a home that was never mine.
~ only if you'd come back

*If you want to be accepted for who you are
you must forgive yourself your imperfections.*

Humility is a trait that comes naturally to those who find neither arrogance in hierarchy nor ease in opulence.

Some rely on measure others are accustomed to estimate,
yet each man masters his own brew.

*In the circus of life
it is therapeutic to play clown now and then.*

*Those that revere not the deep
have only trodden shallow waters.*

Cast your net with a lot of faith;
catch a shoal with little bait.

*Too many strings attached
makes a puppet of man.*

*Even those with perfect eyesight
are partial by vision.*

*A house in shambles
is indicative of foundations week.*

*Outside the temple a beggar sat
waiting for God to reward his faith.*

*Gift not a bouquet to one who recognizes not
the fragrance of a flower.*

When desire rotates to conspire
a treacherous gamble unfolds.

*Blurred eyes made a wish
and compelled the heavens to see.*

Winged grace flutter near,
for butterflies like demons dance
and you are the hope midst the fear.

*In the symphony of existence,
embrace the dissonance as much as the harmony,
for both compose the melody of life."*

In the tapestry of life,
love remains the most enchanting mystery,
weaving threads of passion, connection,
and understanding into
the sublime masterpiece
of the human heart."

The bee's hum echoes the poetry of purpose,
and the flower's bloom whispers
the secrets swathed in sweetness."

*Entitled to serve, constricted by the doors of reality
he suffocated the dreams of glee to survive.*

I would buy a fortune,
if only it was to be sold in the shops of preachers.

I sit amidst the calm, on a bench of fragility,
and witness the havoc my mind creates.

Divine is the grace of solitude,
the epitome of resilience that far from the crowd
scrutinizes the soul.

*The verses of you are etched in my mind
like a poignant echo defying time.*

*And though the world may cast its stones with scorn,
remember, love can bloom where petals are burn.*

What hurts now, once was the glory I carried;
what I want to forget now,
once I wished to capture forever.
It's not the memories, not the people,
it's the dynamics of time
no one could ever surpass.

The paradox of presence,
a ghost in the throng,
Where connection's embraced
feels distant and long.

A tapestry of scars, beneath my skin,
Whispers of goodbyes where love had been.
The echo of a trust, so recklessly given,
Shattered like glass, a love unforgiving.

There's still life after the threshold,
things once begun surely end;
But what's meant to be, will be,
and such is the magic of life.